I play for Port .

The kit is wicked!
Too cool to mess up!

Bit by bit I get ready to play.

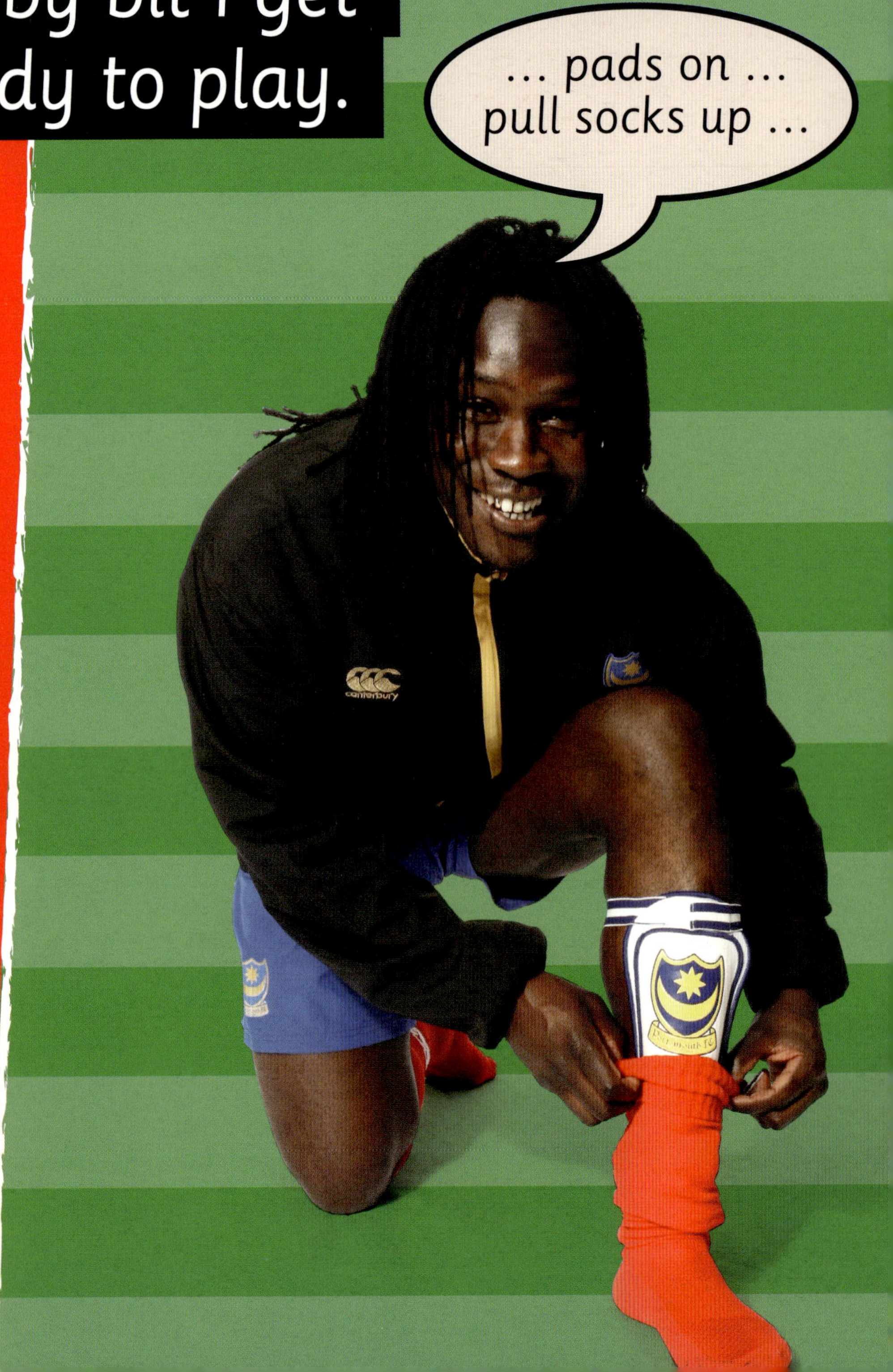
... pads on ...
pull socks up ...

Ahhh! No!! Not *lots* of boots! Two will do!

… put boots on …

… unzip jacket.

Jacket off, and ...

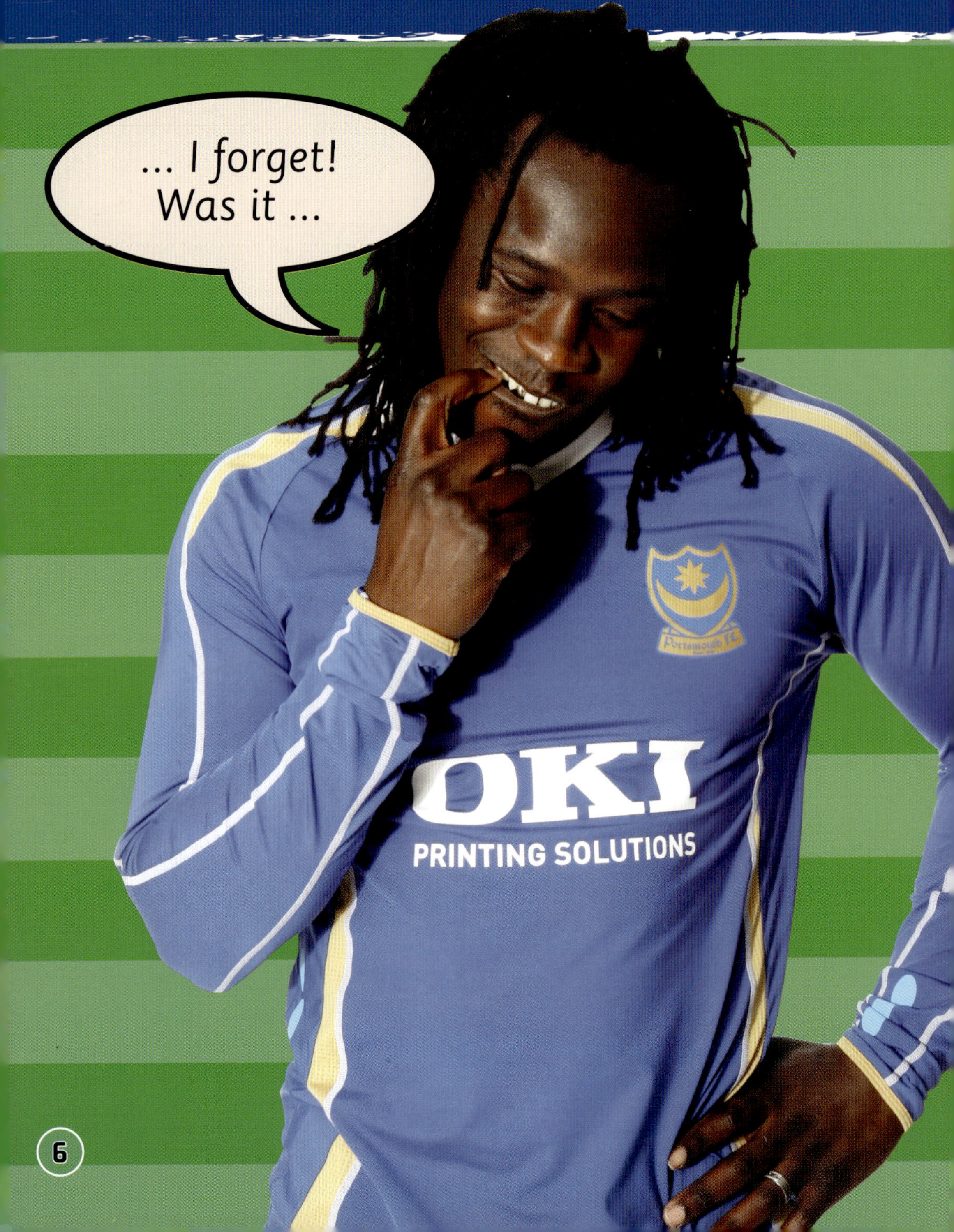
... I forget!
Was it ...
OKI
PRINTING SOLUTIONS

... a hat?

Uhh!? No way!
No hats.
Not cool!
OKI
PRINTING SOLUTIONS

I'm not ready to play yet!

... tuck top in.

Yes! Top, shorts, socks, pads and boots. Now I'm ready to play!

Ah! No, I forgot … and a ball!

Toss the ball up!

Now I'm ready to win!
And get a hat trick?
You bet!